SPAIN

Jim Knable

BROADWAY PLAY PUBLISHING INC
224 E 62nd St, NY NY 10065-8201
212 772-8334 fax: 212 772-8358
BroadwayPlayPubl.com

SPAIN
© Copyright 2007 by Jim Knable

1st printing: October 2007, 2nd printing: June 2011
I S B N: 978-0-88145-367-6

Book design: Marie Donovan
Word processing: Microsoft Word
Typographic controls: Ventura Publisher
Typeface: Palatino
Printed and bound in the U S A

ABOUT THE AUTHOR

Jim Knable's plays have been produced at M C C
Theater, N Y C's Summer Play Festival (2006),
The Woolly Mammoth Theater, Soho Rep, Playwrights
Theater of New Jersey, New Jersey Rep, Actor's Express
in Atlanta, Phoenix Theater of Indianapolis, Yale
University, and N Y U. Commissioned and produced
touring educational plays for Playwrights Project and
The Hangar Theater. He began his playwriting career as
a teenager, winning the California Young Playwrights
Contest three times and the National Young
Playwrights Contest twice. His other plays
include GREEN MAN, THE RAPIER OF EUROPA,
OTHAMLET, and TRUE AND SOLID GROUND.

Jim is also a songwriter and leader of the N Y C band
The Randy Bandits, who released the album *Redbeard*
in 2006.

SPAIN received its professional premiere on
10 December 2001 at the Woolly Mammoth Theater
Company, Washington DC (Howard Shalwitz,
Artistic Director; Kevin Moore, Managing Director).
The cast and creative contributors were:

BARBARA .... Emily Townley
CONQUISTADOR .... Chris Lane
ANCIENT *et al* .... Sarah Marshall
JOHN *et al* .... Andrew Wynn
DIVERSION .... Katie Barrett

Director .... Tom Prewitt
Sets .... Robin Stapley
Lights .... Lisa Ogonowski
Costumes .... Rosemary Pardee
Sound .... Dave McKeever
Props .... Linda Evans
Dramaturg .... Mary Resing
Stage manager .... Margie Hasmall

SPAIN received its New York City premiere on
18 July 2006 at The Summer Play Festival (Arielle
Tepper, Producer and Founder). The cast and creative
contributors were:

BARBARA . . . . Stephanie Kurtzuba
CONQUISTADOR . . . . Michael Aronov
ANCIENT *et al* . . . . Lisa Barnes
JOHN *et al* . . . . David Rossmer
DIVERSION . . . . Barb Pitts

Director . . . . Jeremy Dobrish
Sets . . . . Dustin O'Neill
Lights . . . . Michael Gottlieb
Costumes . . . . Jessica Ford
Sound . . . . Jill B C DuBoff
Stage manager . . . . Alexis R Prussack

SPAIN received its Off-Broadway Premiere on
10 October 2007 at M C C Theater, New York City
(Bernard Telsey and Robert LuPone, Artistic Directors;
William Cantler, Associate Artistic Director; Blake
West, Executive Director). The cast and creative
contributors were:

BARBARA .... Annabella Sciorra
CONQUISTADOR .... Michael Aronov
ANCIENT *et al* .... Lisa Kron
JOHN *et al* .... Erik Jensen
DIVERSION .... Veanne Cox

Director .... Jeremy Dobrish
Sets .... Beowulf Boritt
Lights .... Michael Gottlieb
Costumes .... Jenny Mannis
Sound .... Jill B C DuBoff
Props .... Jeremy Lydi
Stage manager .... Alexis R Prussac

CHARACTERS & SETTING

BARBARA, *a woman in her thirties*

CONQUISTADOR, *a barbarous man in armor in his thirties or forties*

ANCIENT, *also* OLD MAN, ROMAN, LAWYER, MONK, PSYCHIATRIST, GENERAL. *A woman in her fifties playing men's roles.*

DIVERSION, *a woman in her thirties. A little older than* BARBARA. *No wiser.*

JOHN, BARBARA's *husband. Also* GUITAR PLAYER, SHEPHERD *and* HORSE.

The time is the present. Sort of.

For Rosey, my partner in time

In memory of Stewart Fisher

1

(BARBARA and CONQUISTADOR are on opposite sides of the stage, unaware of each other.)

BARBARA: The heart of Spain is gold. Warm. Welcoming. Culture and cultures mixing, glowing in the high heat of the noon day sun.

CONQUISTADOR: The discovery of the New World marked a major turning point in my life. It opened up doors, gave me options I never knew I had. I found a genuine sense of purpose. I really felt like I was doing something for a change.

BARBARA: The soul of Spain.

CONQUISTADOR: Conquering. It is a great feeling. Meeting uncivilized people. Killing them, making them your slaves, what not.

BARBARA: Roosters.

CONQUISTADOR: For the first time in my life, I felt good about myself. My parents were proud of me. My wife wanted to sleep with me all the time.

BARBARA: Flamenco.

CONQUISTADOR: She told me I had become so much more virile. It was true.

BARBARA: The sweet sea smell of Barcelona.

CONQUISTADOR: My sexual appetite was insatiable. And I sated it quite often. Usually with my wife.

BARBARA: Red and Black and Yellow.

CONQUISTADOR: Ah, the New World, the new me.

BARBARA: Ferdinand and Isabella.

CONQUISTADOR: This helmet.

BARBARA: Picasso.

CONQUISTADOR: This beautiful shiny thing.

BARBARA: Gaudi.

CONQUISTADOR: Sometimes at night, I just sit on my bed and hold it on my lap.

BARBARA: Dali.

CONQUISTADOR: Trace the engraving. Look at my face in the reflection.

BARBARA: Lorca.

CONQUISTADOR: Who else gets to wear something like this?

BARBARA: Art.

CONQUISTADOR: The Spanish blood is strong in our veins.

BARBARA: Music.

CONQUISTADOR: We go places and name them.

BARBARA: Fire in the belly. Nothing else like it.

CONQUISTADOR: And in the heat of battle. On my horse. This God-like thing on my head. I swing my sword down. I feel so...good. Really and truly good. Blessed.

BARBARA: I have never been to Spain.

CONQUISTADOR: And afterwards. Wipe off the blood, get off my horse, stick my feet in the new earth, drink with my friends, maybe rape a prisoner.

BARBARA: I don't know Spanish.

CONQUISTADOR: This is what I was made for. I believe that. Look at me. This is who I am. I love myself.

BARBARA: The heart of Spain is gold.

(A GUITAR PLAYER *appears, playing a fast Spanish dance song.* BARBARA *dances in place, facing the audience. Conquistador does the same. They stop. The guitar stops.)*

BARBARA: I first hallucinated him shortly after my husband of five years left me for some slut with a boob job.

(Lights reveal CONQUISTADOR *sitting on a sofa with his feet up.)*

BARBARA: He was sitting on my sofa with his feet up. His funny metal boots on my coffee table. I was not attracted to him in the traditional sense.
    I knew immediately he was not a real human being. He looked like one, smelled like one; when he talked I heard his voice like I'd hear anyone else's. But he was quite obviously a delusionary fragment of a repressed childhood primal picture book memory, nothing more.
    I asked him: Who are you?

CONQUISTADOR: They call me El Tigre.

BARBARA: I asked him: Why are you here?

CONQUISTADOR: I do not know. It is a great mystery to me.

BARBARA: I asked him: What century are you from?

CONQUISTADOR: Sixteenth, year of our Lord, bless us and protect us, amen.

BARBARA: I did not ask him about his profession. Obviously he was a Conquistador. A real Spanish Conquistador. Luckily, he spoke English.

I did ask him to take his metal boots off my coffee table. And if I could take his sword and helmet.

CONQUISTADOR: *(Taking his boots off the coffee table)*
I will hold on to them, thank you.

BARBARA: And then I said: Where exactly were you
before this and how do you think you got from that
place to my apartment?

CONQUISTADOR: It is a strange story.

BARBARA: I called in sick to work. *(to him)* I want to
hear it.

(GUITAR PLAYER strums.)

CONQUISTADOR: Well... *(Stands)* It was a raid like any
other. Screaming, burning dwellings, what not. We
rode through this...I suppose you could call it an alley
or street...past the charred huts and dead Indians. And
we came to an odd structure. A temple of sorts. We had
seen it from a distance. A pyramid of sorts. Very tall,
many steps. We all liked the look of it and decided
not to destroy it. We would instead use it to throw
a festival. It was perfect.
    I got off my horse with the others and climbed all
those steps. I could hear my men behind me. Clomp,
clomp, clomp. The air grew cooler, the breeze blew
lightly. I came to a portal. An entrance. Inside, a fire
was glowing. I walked in. I saw an ancient sitting
before the fire.

*(CONQUISTADOR walks left, into a new space. An implied
fire is on the ground. An ANCIENT sits before it. Silence.
ANCIENT and CONQUISTADOR look at each other.)*

ANCIENT: *Buenas noches.*

*(CONQUISTADOR draws his sword and prepares to strike.
He stops, suddenly, to correct.)*

CONQUISTADOR: *Buenos días.*

ANCIENT: *Buenas noches, Señor.*

CONQUISTADOR: *No. Buenos días. (Pointing outside) Días.*

ANCIENT: *No, Señor Tigre. Buenas noches.*

CONQUISTADOR: At which point there was a bright flash
of light like lightening and I saw a vision.
  A man on a skeleton donkey. A monkey's head on
his neck. A crowd of men in white robes and hoods
surrounding him.
  And then I became the man with the monkey head
and the white hoods fell. All their eyes glowed red.
And lion claws reached out from white sleeves to
touch me. And I closed my eyes and heard a voice.

ANCIENT: The Mayan calendar is indicative of the
high level of civilization, intelligence and world
comprehension found within the Mayan culture. Days,
weeks and months are counted as are all numbers with
dots and lines. And on this day of the four dots and two
lines, there is predicted a shift in the very nature of time
and continuity. That is to say, your raid of our culture
was prophesied and you are now to become the vessel
of higher perception due to the fact that I already know
everything and the rest of the village is dead.

(Stage left goes black.)

CONQUISTADOR: And then another flash of light and
I found myself sitting on your furniture. *(Beat)* Where
am I?

BARBARA: We call it the United States of America.

CONQUISTADOR: America?

BARBARA: Yes. Look. Did I hear you say burn and kill
people?

CONQUISTADOR: Savages.

BARBARA: Your sword. Oh God.

CONQUISTADOR: Blood of the savages. I would have
washed it if I knew I was coming.

BARBARA: Suddenly I feel ill.

CONQUISTADOR: Plague?

BARBARA: Conscience. What an awful hallucination.

CONQUISTADOR: You are having a vision now?

BARBARA: I like Spain. I love Spain.

CONQUISTADOR: Good, I won't have to kill you.

BARBARA: But you represent everything I hate about Spain and mankind in general.

CONQUISTADOR: I don't understand you.

BARBARA: You are symbolic of fear and repression and colonization and everything evil.

CONQUISTADOR: Evil?

BARBARA: But I love Spain. Jesus. Why couldn't you have been Lorca or Picasso. Well no, not Picasso.

CONQUISTADOR: I am not evil.

BARBARA: Cervantes.

CONQUISTADOR: I am all good.

BARBARA: Dali.

CONQUISTADOR: I love myself.

BARBARA: I don't want to deal with this right now.

CONQUISTADOR: I'm not even going to rape you.

BARBARA: And that's when I left.

(Black on all but BARBARA *and* DIVERSION, *her best friend.)*

DIVERSION: Barbara, I'm worried about you.

BARBARA: You're always worried about me.

DIVERSION: I'm always concerned. Now I am worried, this is worry.

BARBARA: You don't believe me?

DIVERSION: I do. I truly believe you are delusional.

BARBARA: But why him? Of all the delusions...

DIVERSION: Do you need to come live with me?

BARBARA: What?

DIVERSION: Being alone so suddenly. You're not used to being alone. And the circumstances.

BARBARA: I don't want to live with you.

(Beat)

DIVERSION: Why not?

BARBARA: I have a place. I live in a place. I'm okay.

DIVERSION: You're having conversations with conquistadors!

BARBARA: I shouldn't have told you.

DIVERSION: Why not? I'm your best friend.

BARBARA: It's not like I'm doing harm to myself.

DIVERSION: You're missing work.

BARBARA: I hate work.

DIVERSION: No, you don't.

BARBARA: I do. I really do. I'm sick of Escrow folders and phone calls to buyers and Roman with his goatee and his roaming hands. I want to quit.

DIVERSION: Quit? Quit and do what?

BARBARA: Go to Spain.

DIVERSION: You're obsessive.

BARBARA: You should encourage me.

DIVERSION: You don't even know Spanish.

BARBARA: Maybe the Conquistador will teach me.

(Silence)

DIVERSION: I have to get back to work. Do you want me to say anything to Roman?

BARBARA: No, no. I already told him I was sick in bed.

DIVERSION: That's not the only place you're sick.

BARBARA: Go back to work. I'll call you tonight.

(DIVERSION *disappears. Lights shift.* CONQUISTADOR *is sitting with his helmet in his lap on the sofa. He looks at his face in its reflection.* BARBARA *stands above him.*)

BARBARA: You're still here.

CONQUISTADOR: Yes.

BARBARA: What are you doing?

CONQUISTADOR: Spending time with my helmet. It makes me feel peaceful.

BARBARA: Your helmet?

CONQUISTADOR: Yes. Look. Come look.

(BARBARA *walks cautiously over to* CONQUISTADOR *and sits beside him on the sofa. They look at the helmet together.*)

BARBARA: What are these designs?

CONQUISTADOR: Beautiful, no?

BARBARA: Yes. But what are they?

CONQUISTADOR: Tigers.

(*He looks up at her and smiles.*)

BARBARA: El Tigre.

CONQUISTADOR: Sí.

(*Silence*)

BARBARA: I know that if I touched you, I would actually feel you.

CONQUISTADOR: I do not understand.

BARBARA: I know it without even trying. And I know I don't want to try.

CONQUISTADOR: To try what?

BARBARA: To touch you.

(CONQUISTADOR *looks at* BARBARA. *He places his hand on her breast.*)

CONQUISTADOR: Like this?

BARBARA: *(Pushing his hand away quickly)* Don't. I don't want that.

CONQUISTADOR: I am beginning to.

(BARBARA *stands and moves away from him.*)

Do not be afraid. I would not dishonor you without your permission.

BARBARA: You're a killer and a rapist.

CONQUISTADOR: Only with Savages.

BARBARA: They're not savages, they're human beings and you wiped them out of existence.

CONQUISTADOR: Where is your husband? *(Silence. He holds up a photo frame with a picture of* BARBARA *and a man in it.)* This painting. I found it in your bedroom. Very true to life, especially for a miniature.

BARBARA: It's a photograph. I'm not going to explain what that is.

CONQUISTADOR: This is your husband, is it not?

(Beat)

BARBARA: It was.

CONQUISTADOR: He's dead?

(Beat)

BARBARA: Yes.

CONQUISTADOR: He was killed in battle?

(BARBARA *laughs.* CONQUISTADOR *looks at her.*)

BARBARA: John never fought a battle in his life.

CONQUISTADOR: He was lame?

BARBARA: Yes, he was very lame. Lame, boring, cowardly, lying, cheating.

CONQUISTADOR: How did he die? Did somebody kill him?

(BARBARA *looks at* CONQUISTADOR's *sword.*)

BARBARA: I killed him.

CONQUISTADOR: You?

BARBARA: Sure. I found him with another woman and killed both of them.

(*Silence*)

CONQUISTADOR: Hm. Good. Did you kill them in sleep?

BARBARA: No. I killed them in the heat of their passion.

CONQUISTADOR: Good. Good.

BARBARA: You approve?

CONQUISTADOR: I would do the same to my wife if I found her with another.

BARBARA: Would you rape her first?

CONQUISTADOR: (*Repulsed*) No. No. She's my wife.

BARBARA: Give me that picture.

(BARBARA *holds out her hand.* CONQUISTADOR *hands it to her.*)

CONQUISTADOR: Why do you still keep it?

(BARBARA *looks at him. She smashes the frame against the table, takes out the photo and rips it to shreds. Silence*)

CONQUISTADOR: You are not going to stomp and spit on it?

(Beat. BARBARA does so.)

CONQUISTADOR: How do you feel?

(BARBARA looks at him.)

BARBARA: Savage.

(Blackout)

ANCIENT: *(V O)* The position of Ancient in a community is one to be acquired only through perseverance, bravery and self-mastery. It is a position of supreme wisdom beyond all comprehension. Most Ancients are destined to be Ancient from birth. All they have to do is live long enough.
    And then there is the question of madness.

(Lights up on the full stage. The ANCIENT stands omnisciently. The GUITAR PLAYER plays flamenco bursts. BARBARA has CONQUISTADOR's sword. She is practicing sword thrusts, lunging in place while CONQUISTADOR stands behind her, steadying her arm, his other arm at her waist.)

ANCIENT: Madness and wisdom are necessary brothers. Wisdom does not rise from sanity. Madness does not result from ignorance. Madness is more ancient than wisdom. I eat hay and howl at the sun every morning.

CONQUISTADOR: Good. It is in your nature

BARBARA: It is?

CONQUISTADOR: I am sure you dealt a swift and cruel death to your husband.

(BARBARA stops.)

BARBARA: What am I doing?

CONQUISTADOR: Reliving the death blow. You thrust your sword into him, his blood spilled in rivers on the ground. His head went rolling down the stone steps.

BARBARA: I don't have stone steps.

CONQUISTADOR: You took your bloody revenge at the peak of his betrayal.

BARBARA: Betrayal. Yes, right, I did.

CONQUISTADOR: Did he see you come in?

BARBARA: No. No, not at first. She saw me. She screamed. The sword went through his back and came out his chest. His mouth fell open. This is horrible. Am I saying this?

CONQUISTADOR: Yes, yes, tell me more.

BARBARA: I never killed anyone.

CONQUISTADOR: It is a great feeling, is it not? The power.

BARBARA: Power. Yes. Having the power to...kill him. Kill him. (*She thrusts.*)

CONQUISTADOR: Yes!

BARBARA: Stab him through the heart!

CONQUISTADOR: It is beautiful!

BARBARA: Destroy him!

CONQUISTADOR: You have so much Duende! You are so strong!

(*She stops.*)

BARBARA: I am? I have what?

CONQUISTADOR: Duende. I want to take my armor off with you.

BARBARA: I don't think that's a good idea.

CONQUISTADOR: You would like to remove it for me.

BARBARA: We'd better keep the armor on in this relationship.

CONQUISTADOR: I am holding you around the waist.

BARBARA: Yes.

CONQUISTADOR: Why are you letting me?

(BARBARA *pulls out a phone and speaks out to* DIVERSION.)

BARBARA: And I couldn't really answer. But there was no denying it. Since he came, I had destroyed my husband's picture, allowed him to put his cold hand on my breast and held his sword.

(DIVERSION *is lit, standing with a phone while the* ANCIENT *gives her a metaphysical shoulder massage.*)

DIVERSION: You touched him.

BARBARA: We've touched each other.

DIVERSION: You're not supposed to be able to touch delusions.

BARBARA: That's what I'm trying to tell you. This is turning into something else.

DIVERSION: Roman asked about you.

BARBARA: Are you hearing me?

DIVERSION: He asked if you were really sick or if you were planning to quit soon.

BARBARA: I don't care.

DIVERSION: I told him he would have to ask you himself tomorrow. When you come in.

BARBARA: Do you want to meet the Conquistador?

DIVERSION: I'll be right there.

(BARBARA *hangs up. Dark on* DIVERSION.)

CONQUISTADOR: You can communicate with spirits?

BARBARA: What?

CONQUISTADOR: You were not talking to me, but when you were talking I thought I heard a small voice near us.

BARBARA: I was using a telephone. It was invented by Alexander Graham Bell. It lets people talk to each other without them having to be in the same place.

CONQUISTADOR: Why would anyone want to do that?

BARBARA: I don't know.

CONQUISTADOR: I do not feel that you have told me exactly where I am.

BARBARA: This is the future. You're a few hundred years past where you were before this.

CONQUISTADOR: Are you part of my vision?

BARBARA: You are part of mine.

(A doorbell rings. CONQUISTADOR jumps back and grabs his sword.)

BARBARA: It's all right. That was my doorbell. It's Diversion.

CONQUISTADOR: I don't understand.

BARBARA: My best friend. Diversion.

CONQUISTADOR: What does that mean?

BARBARA: Don't worry about it. You're about to meet her.

(BARBARA opens the door.)

(DIVERSION steps in and yells at seeing the CONQUISTADOR.)

(CONQUISTADOR yells back.)

(Stunned silence)

DIVERSION: My God.

BARBARA: I told you.

DIVERSION: I'm seeing your delusion.

BARBARA: Two people can't see the same delusion.

DIVERSION: Can I touch him?

BARBARA: Can she?

CONQUISTADOR: Please.

(DIVERSION *touches him.*)

DIVERSION: Oh! My God. Look at him. His metal is cold.

BARBARA: His hands are cold.

DIVERSION: What about his face?

BARBARA: I don't know.

(DIVERSION *reaches out and touches* CONQUISTADOR's *face. She holds her hand there.*)

DIVERSION: Oh...

BARBARA: Cold?

DIVERSION: Warm. Hot. Burning. (*She pulls her hand back gently.*) Where did you come from?

CONQUISTADOR: It is a strange story.

DIVERSION: I want to hear it.

(CONQUISTADOR *looks at* BARBARA.)

BARBARA: Go on. Tell it. I'll get us drinks. What would you like?

DIVERSION: Jim Beam on the rocks.

BARBARA: I'll be right back.

(BARBARA *exits.* GUITAR PLAYER *strums.*)

CONQUISTADOR: It was a day like any other. Roaming the green fields of my countryside. Alone on my

stallion. Crossing short wooden bridges over brooks.
I came to a grove of trees and bushes. Beneath one tree
sat an old man. I swung off my horse and stood before
him.

(CONQUISTADOR *walks; lights follow him. The* ANCIENT
sits on the ground, leaning up against an implied tree.)

CONQUISTADOR: *Buenos días.*

ANCIENT: *A las cinco de la tarde.*

CONQUISTADOR: *Que?*

ANCIENT: *El niño come naranjas.*

CONQUISTADOR: And all at once there was burst of light
and I saw a vision.
  A woman dressed in a flowing white gown, her hair
falling down on her shoulders. Floating above the
earth. Her lips move as if to speak, but I hear nothing.
A dew drop. A lily shaft open. The crowning of a boy
eating oranges.
  And then another burst of light and I was here. And
the woman I knew in her white dress was dressed like
a man.

(*Lights up on stage right.* BARBARA *stands nonplussed with
two drinks.*)

BARBARA: That wasn't the story you told me.

DIVERSION: It was beautiful.

BARBARA: What happened to killing and raping
everybody?

(CONQUISTADOR *just looks at* BARBARA.)

DIVERSION: Barbara. Don't offend him. He would never
do that. He is a knight. A noble knight.

BARBARA: He's a Conquistador!

DIVERSION: You are his Dulcinea. You are his lady in white.

BARBARA: What happened while I was in the kitchen?

CONQUISTADOR: I told the story of my journey here, my lady.

BARBARA: My lady? Now I'm my lady?

DIVERSION: He is quite obviously in love with you.

BARBARA: What happened to you? You were against this whole thing being real at all.

DIVERSION: People can change.

BARBARA: Stop. Stop.

(BARBARA *passes the drinks off to* DIVERSION *and walks up to* CONQUISTADOR.)

BARBARA: What have you done to my friend?

CONQUISTADOR: I told her my story.

BARBARA: Why does she get a different story than I do?

CONQUISTADOR: She is a different woman.

BARBARA: So she gets the pretty story about countrysides and brooks and I get the pillaging and burning story.
   She gets a woman in a white dress and I get you on a skeleton donkey with a monkey head? I'm the one in mourning for something! I'm the one who needs soothing!

CONQUISTADOR: Mourning?

BARBARA: I'm stranded. I'm alone. My husband left me for a slut with a boob job.

CONQUISTADOR: You killed your husband and his lover.

DIVERSION: Barbara?

BARBARA: I didn't kill them. I just told you I did to make myself feel good.

(*Silence.* BARBARA *and* CONQUISTADOR *look at each other.*)

CONQUISTADOR: Did it feel good?

BARBARA: Yes.

DIVERSION: What is he talking about, Barbara?

(*Beat.* BARBARA *turns to* DIVERSION.)

BARBARA: He's talking about murder. He's talking about lust. He's talking about wind that blows over the heads of the dead. He is a cruel, barbaric man with a bloody sword at his waist, a hundred angry souls at his heels and desire stronger than anything you've ever known in his heart.

DIVERSION: Am I dreaming?

BARBARA: You don't belong here.

DIVERSION: Does he?

BARBARA: Yes. But only as I want him.

DIVERSION: Barbara, am I losing my mind?

BARBARA: No. You're the sane one. Go home and pretend you dreamt this. Leave the drinks for us. Go.

(DIVERSION *exits.* BARBARA *looks at* CONQUISTADOR.)

BARBARA: What are you, really?

CONQUISTADOR: What do you believe?

BARBARA: I don't know what to think.

CONQUISTADOR: Do not think.

BARBARA: Who do you think I am?

CONQUISTADOR: I am not thinking.

BARBARA: A woman in man's clothing? A vision?

CONQUISTADOR: Yes.

BARBARA: Which story is true?

CONQUISTADOR: Both.

(A brilliant flash of white light. The ANCIENT *stands and sings with the* GUITAR PLAYER. *The* GUITAR PLAYER *in Spanish, the* ANCIENT *in English.)*

(As they sing BARBARA *begins removing* CONQUISTADOR's *armor with his help and silent instruction. This is not erotic. It is simple.)*

GUITAR PLAYER:	ANCIENT:
En mita del mar	Out in the sea
había una piedra	was a stone.
y se sentaba mi compaerita	My girl sat down
a contarle sus penas	to tell it her pains.
Tan solamente a la Tierra	Only to the Earth
le cuento lo que me pasa,	do I tell my troubles,
porque en el mundo no encuentro	for nowhere in the world
persona e mi confianza	do I find anyone I trust.

*(*CONQUISTADOR *stands in his Sixteenth Century underwear.* BARBARA *motions for him to sit on the floor by the table. She pulls a bottle of whiskey out from under the table, drinks from it. He drinks. She drinks. He drinks.)*

*(*BARBARA *reaches under the table and pulls out a large travel book. She opens it and shows it to* CONQUISTADOR.*)*

BARBARA: It's been my fantasy for a long time.

CONQUISTADOR: Spain.

BARBARA: I wanted to go there with John. I wanted that to be the place where we found love again. I wanted a country to love.

CONQUISTADOR: You want love.

BARBARA: Wanted.

CONQUISTADOR: And now?

BARBARA: Tell me what it feels like to kill someone.

CONQUISTADOR: You already know.

BARBARA: A whole civilization. What is that like?

CONQUISTADOR: It is like nothing else.

BARBARA: It makes you feel strong.

CONQUISTADOR: Yes.

BARBARA: Because they can't defend themselves against your weapons.

CONQUISTADOR: Yes.

BARBARA: And you can do anything you want with them?

CONQUISTADOR: Yes.

(BARBARA *drinks.*)

BARBARA: Cut off their heads.

CONQUISTADOR: Of course.

BARBARA: Disembowel them.

CONQUISTADOR: Certainly.

BARBARA: Cut off their balls.

CONQUISTADOR: Occasionally.

BARBARA: You ride into town with your men,
in your armor; you all stink like horses...

CONQUISTADOR: Horses, oh yes!

BARBARA: The villagers stare up at you terrified,
helpless, you don't even see them as human...

CONQUISTADOR: Villagers?

BARBARA: The weak, the peasants...

CONQUISTADOR: Peasants, pthuh...

BARBARA: Then what?

CONQUISTADOR: Kill the peasants!

BARBARA: Yes! You hit your heels on your horse and ride through them, swooping your sword, hacking, slashing...

CONQUISTADOR: *(Suggesting)* Chopping?

BARBARA: Chopping up and down!
  You take up a fiery lance, you hurl it through the air, it soars, fire trailing, down into the hut where the men hold ceremonies; it bursts into flames.

CONQUISTADOR: Many, many flames!

BARBARA: You burn it all down, you leave nothing standing. The dirt roads run muddy with blood.

CONQUISTADOR: Muddy blood.

BARBARA: You drink the blood, your mouth is red, you run, screaming battle cries, killing everything in your path, even your own men, your lust consumes you.

CONQUISTADOR: You are very good at this.

BARBARA: You burn with death and pain, painless pain because you feel nothing but overpowering joy, you spin your arms and wave your sword and stand on top off all the bodies, like a mountain, you stand on top and breathe in the smell of torn-out flesh!

(CONQUISTADOR drinks.)

CONQUISTADOR: Yes, all that. I do that. This drink is good. What is it?

BARBARA: Whiskey.
  John drank it, his bottle.

BARBARA:	CONQUISTADOR:
(Gleefully, with him)	*(As before with the portrait)*
Why do I still keep it?	Why do you still keep it?

(She takes another swig and hurls it offstage.)

(Crash!)

(They laugh.)

BARBARA: I could destroy everything.
   The couch. We bought it together.

(BARBARA *goes to the couch and tears into the pillows, hurling them, violent and crazy.* CONQUISTADOR *helps some, but is no match for her fury.)*

BARBARA: What else? More pictures? I have more pictures. Dishes? The sheets? His smell still on them. Everything here we had together, I could destroy everything!

CONQUISTADOR: You are amazing.

BARBARA: I could destroy, myself, I could destroy... I could... *(She flops down on the remains of the couch.)* Too much, too fast. Spinning.

CONQUISTADOR: Spinning. Yes, spinning your arms.

BARBARA: Room spinning.
   Can't look.
   Too much... *(She collapses.)*

CONQUISTADOR: Barbara?

(Lights rise on the ANCIENT, *fall on* CONQUISTADOR *and* BARBARA.*)*

(While the ANCIENT *talks, he changes into a very corporate looking business suit.)*

ANCIENT: There is always the question of violence.
   Violence can come from outside or inside. *(Pause)*
   Occasionally, it is necessary to make a sacrifice.

The Ancient will choose who to sacrifice.
Take him to the temple. Tie him to the rock.
Hold the point of the blade over his heart and
then...push it in.
There is usually screaming and spattering of blood.
This is to be expected. No one likes to be sacrificed.
But then the sky opens up along a bright white crack.
The moon is invented. The dark grass of hills holding
trees waves in sea green, the whole of souls goes
spinning; and names are remembered. Empires fall.
Countries lose their borders. Anything is then possible.
All are capable of such violence.

(Light falls on ANCIENT. *Rises on* CONQUISTADOR *and*
BARBARA. *Morning. They are sleeping, passed out on the*
floor.

(A key in a lock is heard.)

(A door swings open.)

*(*JOHN *[the* GUITAR PLAYER*] walks on carrying a guitar*
in a case and a trunk full of his clothes. He looks spent
and dejected. At first he does not see BARBARA *and*
CONQUISTADOR. *He lays down his load and flops onto*
the couch. Now he notices the bodies. He peers at them
inquisitively. He notices the armor lying near the table.)

JOHN: Barbara? Barbara?

BARBARA: *(In sleep)* John?

JOHN: Barbara, I'm back. I'm sorry I left you. What is
this man doing on the floor and why is there armor in
our house?

BARBARA: John? *(She wakes.)* John?! *(Sitting bolt upright)*
John?!!

JOHN: You wouldn't believe what I've been through.
And now this. Christ, what a strange world.

BARBARA: What are you doing here?

JOHN: Yolanda dumped me for some guy with big muscles and no neck. I realized I made a mistake leaving you. I came back. I hope you can forgive me. Do you want to tell me who this guy is?

BARBARA: You're gone.

JOHN: I'm right here.

BARBARA: I killed you.

JOHN: Honey, I think you're still a little bit asleep.

BARBARA: I walked in on you and the slut with the boob job having sex in our bed and I slaughtered you both.

JOHN: Barbara, I 'm right here. I'm alive. Yolanda's alive. I wish she was dead, but she's alive. You're in the middle of a dream or something.

BARBARA: Spain.

JOHN: What?

BARBARA: Spain. *(She stands.)*

JOHN: You want to talk about Spain right now? Why don't you go splash some water on your face. Would you like me to make coffee?

(BARBARA walks over to the armor and picks up the sword.)

JOHN: What are you doing? Jesus, what the hell is that?

BARBARA: Spain.

(BARBARA puts the point of the sword against JOHN's chest.)

JOHN: Honey, what are you going to do here? Kill me?

BARBARA: Sure.

(BARBARA drives the sword into JOHN. Lights go white. A phone rings. Black)

BARBARA: Hello?

(Lights back on. DIVERSION *stands next to* ROMAN
*[*ANCIENT*] stage left.* DIVERSION *holds the phone.*
BARBARA *stands calmly with the sword at her side,*
her dead bleeding husband on the sofa and the
CONQUISTADOR *passed out on the floor.)*

DIVERSION: Barbara, it's me. I'm standing here with
Roman. We're both worried about you.

BARBARA: Concerned?

DIVERSION: Worried. I had the strangest dream about
you last night. I was telling Roman about it. Why aren't
you coming into work?

ROMAN: Let me talk to her.

DIVERSION: Roman wants to talk to you.

ROMAN: Barbara, look, I'm not angry with you for lying
about being sick. You're obviously going through
some period of mental instability resulting from being
rejected by your husband. I understand. I've read lots
of books where that happens. But we need you here,
Barbara. We need you in Escrow, we need you on the
phone, we need your magic touch. I think it might even
help you with your feelings of worthlessness to come
in and make yourself busy. I've heard that it's good for
people in your state to keep going to work and, in fact,
work even harder than usual to make up for the
emptiness in their lives. And look, Barbara, I don't
want to have to threaten you, but if you don't come
in by tomorrow, I'll fire you. So why don't you come
in today. What do you say?

BARBARA: I quit.

ROMAN: Barbara, don't do this.

BARBARA: If I came into that office, I would hack all of
you to pieces with a long and blood-stained Spanish
sword.

ROMAN: Maybe you should think about this for a little while. I'll call back tomorrow.

BARBARA: If you call me, I'll track you down and murder your whole family.

ROMAN: Jesus, Barbara, you've really gone off the deep end, haven't you.

BARBARA: Yes.

ROMAN: Well. We'll miss you.

BARBARA: Thanks. Put Diversion on, would you?

ROMAN: No problem. *(Handing* DIVERSION *the phone)* For you. *(He walks off.)*

DIVERSION: What's going on here, Barb?

BARBARA: I'm going through some very important changes.

DIVERSION: Yeah? That sounds positive.

BARBARA: I just quit my job.

DIVERSION: Barbara!

BARBARA: It was easy. It felt good. Just like when I drove this sword into my husband's chest. That's the thing I've realized, you know? It's so easy to simply do these things.

DIVERSION: What are you talking about?

BARBARA: Do you remember your dream from last night? The one with me and the Conquistador? Where he told you what you wanted to hear and I told you the way it was. That really happened. Things like that really happen. Do you understand? No, you probably don't. Why don't you just pretend I'm crazy.

DIVERSION: I think you need help, Barbara.

BARBARA: Good, good.

DIVERSION: I know you have a thing against shrinks, but this guy I've been seeing lately...

BARBARA: I don't care about your personal life. Go give Roman a blow job or something.

DIVERSION: Barbara!

BARBARA: You can use my desk if you like.

DIVERSION: I can't believe...

BARBARA: No, you can't. Good bye.

(BARBARA *hangs up. Dark on* DIVERSION. CONQUISTADOR *is sitting up at this point, watching* BARBARA. *She nods over to* JOHN. CONQUISTADOR *looks at him inquisitively.*)

CONQUISTADOR: Dead.

BARBARA: Dead.

CONQUISTADOR: Who is he?

BARBARA: Husband.

CONQUISTADOR: Again?

BARBARA: Yeah.

CONQUISTADOR: You killed his ghost.

BARBARA: Sure.

CONQUISTADOR: My head hurts.

BARBARA: You have a hang-over.

CONQUISTADOR: Barbara?

BARBARA: *(Jarred at hearing him say her name)* Yeah?

CONQUISTADOR: Why am I still here?

(Beat)

BARBARA: Beats me. But do me a favor. Don't talk like a real human being. *(She starts to walk off.)*

CONQUISTADOR: Where are you going?

BARBARA: Wash the blood off.

(BARBARA *exits. Conquistador looks at John. John opens his eyes and talks nonchalantly to* CONQUISTADOR.)

JOHN: I met Yolanda in a snow storm. I was walking home from the Metro. She was all bundled up like an Eskimo, getting her mail I guess. Very cute. I said something stupid like: Nice snow storm, huh? She laughed. Her breath was hot. It puffed. Then she said: Do you want to come inside? And I thought she was kidding. She couldn't even see my face and I couldn't see hers. But then she took my hand and led me in. All we knew were each other's voices, but she just brought me into her house. And I started to take off my coat but she stopped me, wouldn't even let me take down the hood.

Not yet, she said, and she reached down to her pants and unbuttoned them. And I did the same with mine. And then both of us were standing with no pants or underwear in our big coats and hoods, all bundled up on top. And she pulled me against a wall and we did it like that. The coats, you know, they were squeaking against each other. I put the hole in my hood next to the hole in hers and we breathed on each other. It was like hiding under a blanket. It was wonderful.

When it was over, she said: I will if you will. And we both took off our coats and hoods and laughed and laughed and laughed. Not because we knew each other. Because we didn't.

But then we tried to.

And I left my wife with all her books about Spain and all her misery and boredom.

But then something went wrong.

Something always goes wrong.

And here I am.

Who are you?

CONQUISTADOR: They call me El Tigre. Do you know that you're dead?

(Beat. JOHN *looks down at his body and the blood on his shirt.)*

JOHN: How did that happen?

CONQUISTADOR: Your wife stabbed you.

JOHN: Christ. When?

CONQUISTADOR: Before I woke up.

JOHN: I'm dead?

CONQUISTADOR: Yes.

JOHN: I don't feel dead.

CONQUISTADOR: If she finds you alive, she'll kill you again.

JOHN: Where is she?

CONQUISTADOR: Washing your blood off her hands.

(Beat. JOHN *jumps up.)*

JOHN: I tried, right?

*(*CONQUISTADOR *shrugs.)*

Good luck.

*(*JOHN *runs to his suitcase and guitar, grabs them and leaves.)*

*(*BARBARA *enters, refreshed.* CONQUISTADOR *looks at her.* BARBARA *looks at the empty couch.)*

BARBARA: Where is he?

CONQUISTADOR: He left.

BARBARA: He was dead!

CONQUISTADOR: I told him.

BARBARA: What did he say?

CONQUISTADOR: He told me the story of how he met his lover.

(Beat)

BARBARA: Did he leave through the front door or did angels come and get him or something?

CONQUISTADOR: Front door.

(BARBARA grabs the sword and charges out the front door. CONQUISTADOR sits on the sofa. ANCIENT enters and sits next to CONQUISTADOR. CONQUISTADOR notices, but is not surprised.)

CONQUISTADOR: What am I doing here?

ANCIENT: Being useful.

CONQUISTADOR: When can I leave?

ANCIENT: When you're done.

CONQUISTADOR: Done what?

ANCIENT: Participating in a ritualistic experiment.

CONQUISTADOR: Who are you?

ANCIENT: Ancient.

CONQUISTADOR: Besides that.

ANCIENT: Old man.

CONQUISTADOR: Why do I have two different memories of how I got here?

ANCIENT: They're the same.

CONQUISTADOR: Why won't Barbara sleep with me?

ANCIENT: Because you told her you're a rapist.

(BARBARA enters, sword in hand, out of breath. She sees the ANCIENT.)

BARBARA: Now what.

CONQUISTADOR: Did you find him?

BARBARA: No. I frightened the neighbors. I think someone is going to call the police.

ANCIENT: You must be Barbara.

BARBARA: Yeah. What are you?

CONQUISTADOR: He's the one who sent me here.

BARBARA: Oh.
  You're all-knowing?

ANCIENT: Usually.

BARBARA: How about a little enlightenment?

ANCIENT: You are acting out a Freudian fantasy based on a Jungian nightmare, served to you by an Andalusian Mayan Soul Prophet by way of a delusionary fragment of a repressed childhood primal collective unconscious memory.

BARBARA: You talk like a textbook.

ANCIENT: I have to be going now.

BARBARA & CONQUISTADOR: Wait!

ANCIENT: You'll see me again.

BARBARA: What are we supposed to do?

ANCIENT: Whatever you want.

BARBARA: Is my husband dead or alive?

(ANCIENT *shrugs.*)

BARBARA: Is any of this really happening?

(ANCIENT *nods.*)

BARBARA: Why him?

(*Silence.* CONQUISTADOR *looks at her, a little hurt.* ANCIENT *shakes his head.*)

BARBARA: Am I a murderer?

ANCIENT: No.

BARBARA: Is he?

ANCIENT: Good bye. *(Walks off)*

BARBARA & CONQUISTADOR: Wait!

(Silence. BARBARA and CONQUISTADOR look at each other.)

BARBARA: Put your armor back on.

(Lights move to DIVERSION, who is speaking with her implied psychiatrist.)

DIVERSION: He was dressed in shiny silver metal. It curved around his chest, rose at his shoulders, fell in patterns down his back. His beard was rough and brown. His face was warm, I touched it with my palm. It was so incredibly lifelike. And Barbara was there, too. She was acting crazy, like a wild animal. She tried to make him seem less good. She tried to make him take back the story about the green country and the old man. She doesn't make any sense.
  I tried to suggest she come in and talk to you.

(PSYCHIATRIST [ANCIENT] appears.)

PSYCHIATRIST: Good. That was the right thing to do. Tell me more about the man in shiny silver. Were you attracted to him?

DIVERSION: Not in the traditional sense. There was something familiar about him.

PSYCHIATRIST: You mentioned a story.

DIVERSION: Yes. It was beautiful. He was Don Quixote. But Barbara said he was a Conquistador.

PSYCHIATRIST: How do you feel about Barbara?

DIVERSION: She's lost her marbles.

PSYCHIATRIST: Are you attracted to Barbara?

DIVERSION: I don't want to think about that.

(Lights go stage right. CONQUISTADOR *is back in his armor.)*

BARBARA: We need to make a pact.

CONQUISTADOR: A pact?

BARBARA: A pact between you and me that says we are allies.

CONQUISTADOR: I do not—

BARBARA: Sure you do. Allies. In war. Whatever happens. You protect me, I protect you.

CONQUISTADOR: How will you protect me?

BARBARA: You've seen me in action.

CONQUISTADOR: Yes.

BARBARA: We're in whatever this is together. And I think it's a fight. I think we're fighting something. That's why you're here.

CONQUISTADOR: What are we fighting?

BARBARA: We don't know. Right? But we're here. Look. Give me your sword.

CONQUISTADOR: What are you going to do with it?

BARBARA: Trust me.

*(*CONQUISTADOR *hands her his sword.)*

BARBARA: Get on your knees.

*(*CONQUISTADOR *does so.)*

*(*BARBARA *passes the sword from one of* CONQUISTADOR's *shoulders to the other.)*

BARBARA: I knight you in the name of the fight whatever it is. Rise.

(CONQUISTADOR does. BARBARA hands him the sword.)

BARBARA: Now do it to me.

CONQUISTADOR: I—

(BARBARA gets on her knees.)

BARBARA: Do it.

CONQUISTADOR: I have never met a woman like you.

BARBARA: Sure you have. Knight me.

(Beat. CONQUISTADOR knights BARBARA.)

CONQUISTADOR: I knight you, Barbara—what is your full name?

BARBARA: Tusenbach.

CONQUISTADOR: I knight you Barbara Tusenbach in the name of Spain, Her Majesty, God—

BARBARA: The fight.

CONQUISTADOR: The fight. And in the name of Duende.

BARBARA: Duende? What's that?

CONQUISTADOR: Rise.

(BARBARA rises.)

BARBARA: What's Duende?

(The sound of sirens.)

CONQUISTADOR: What is that noise?

BARBARA: Sirens. They're coming.

CONQUISTADOR: Who?

BARBARA: Our adversaries. What is Duende?

CONQUISTADOR: Everything you cannot name, but already said.

(The sirens get louder.)

BARBARA: Is this what it feels like before a battle?

CONQUISTADOR: Barbara.

BARBARA: Is this the feeling you get? Is this the Duende?

CONQUISTADOR: Barbara Tusenbach.

BARBARA: Yes, El Tigre.

CONQUISTADOR: I have never been in a battle.

BARBARA: What?

CONQUISTADOR: I have never been out of Spain.

BARBARA: What?

CONQUISTADOR: I have never killed anyone.

BARBARA: What are you talking about?

CONQUISTADOR: I wander around the green
countryside pretending. I pretend. I am not even
married.

BARBARA: What the hell are you talking about?!

CONQUISTADOR: I'm pretending this right now.

BARBARA: Bullshit. Bullshit. This is the truest thing
I've ever felt.

CONQUISTADOR: I'm pretending. You're not.

BARBARA: What does that mean?

CONQUISTADOR: I am not a conquistador.

*(A screeching of tires up to a house. A beating on the front
door.)*

COP VOICE: Mrs Tusenbach! Mrs Tusenbach, this is the
police! We have you surrounded. Open up, or we'll
break down your door!

*(BARBARA looks at CONQUISTADOR. She takes his helmet off
his head and puts in on hers. She takes his sword.)*

COP VOICE: Mrs Tusenbach, we know what you've
done! Let us in!

(BARBARA *charges for the door with a terrible battle yell.*)

END OF 1

2

(An interrogation room. BARBARA *sits across from* LAWYER [ANCIENT]. *She is dressed in an orange numbered jumpsuit.)*

LAWYER: Mrs Tusenbach. Let's talk about the carving knife.

BARBARA: What carving knife?

LAWYER: The one you used to attack the policemen at your door and stab your husband.

BARBARA: The Spanish sword?

LAWYER: No. The carving knife. What were you thinking when you picked it up?

BARBARA: The sword?

LAWYER: Sure, the carving knife.

BARBARA: I wasn't thinking.

LAWYER: Were you defending yourself?

BARBARA: I was attacking.

LAWYER: You were attacking your husband and the police.

BARBARA: I was fighting with Duende.

LAWYER: Is Duende the name of the Conquistador?

BARBARA: He's not really a Conquistador.

LAWYER: Let's talk about him.

BARBARA: Who the hell are you, anyway?

LAWYER: I'm your attorney. I introduced myself when I came in. Do you remember that?

BARBARA: Who can believe what anyone says when they introduce themselves?

LAWYER: Mrs Tusenbach, is there a history of mental instability in your family?

BARBARA: No, my family is the only family in the world that acts completely rationally.

LAWYER: You should try to answer my questions cooperatively, Mrs Tusenbach. I'm the one who might save you from a very long prison sentence.

(Beat)

BARBARA: I met him shortly after my husband of five years left me for some slut with a boob job. He was sitting on my sofa with his feet up. His funny metal boots on my coffee table. I was not attracted to him in the traditional sense.

LAWYER: You spoke to him.

BARBARA: It was easy.

LAWYER: Did you think there was anything odd about the situation?

BARBARA: I told him to take his metal boots off my coffee table.

LAWYER: Other than that.

BARBARA: His sword was bloody.

LAWYER: The sword you used to stab your husband and the—

BARBARA: Yes. It was bloody. *(To herself)* How could it be bloody if he wasn't a conquistador? I saw blood.

LAWYER: Whose blood?

BARBARA: Mayan blood. Blood of the people he had slaughtered.

LAWYER: Uh-huh. Go on.

BARBARA: How could I have seen blood if what he said wasn't true?

(Lights switch to down right.)

*(*DIVERSION *stands there holding an orange.)*

DIVERSION: Barbara always was a little, you know, out there. But she controlled it. She worked hard at the office. She was very good at talking to people on the phone and dealing with Escrow. But on her lunch breaks, you know, we would talk, I was her best friend— I am her best friend, and she would say things every once in a while. "I'm feeling restless." "John doesn't pay attention to me." She had this fantasy about Spain. It started two years ago. She saw a movie or something. She started buying books. Maps. She toyed with taking a Spanish class, but she didn't have time and John was very unsupportive of the whole thing.

I don't blame her for stabbing him. He was a real bastard. She shouldn't be punished too harshly for that. I was more disturbed by the other stabbing. That poor man. He was just doing his job. *(She bites into the orange skin and lets the juice run down her chin.)*

(Lights flip over to the table.)

BARBARA: Is that a one-way mirror?

LAWYER: Depends on which side you're on.

*(*BARBARA *stands and walks over to the implied mirror, behind the* LAWYER. *Lights illuminate what she sees in it— the* CONQUISTADOR.)*

LAWYER: What are you going to do? Make faces at them?

(BARBARA *ignores* LAWYER. *She studies the*
CONQUISTADOR. *He is dressed like an Andalusian peasant.*
He mirrors her in a variety of gestures. Finally, their hands
meet where the plane of the mirror would be. They lock
fingers. The LAWYER *watches, fascinated.*)

LAWYER: Barbara?

(CONQUISTADOR *pulls* BARBARA *out of the scene.*
Only they are lit.)

BARBARA: Where are we?

CONQUISTADOR: Green fields. Windmills. Wild horses
and deep bark trees far off.

(BARBARA *takes a moment to look around.*)

BARBARA: It's beautiful. *(Beat)* How did you get out of
my living room?

CONQUISTADOR: White light.

(BARBARA *studies* CONQUISTADOR.)

CONQUISTADOR: Are you angry with me?

BARBARA: *(Laughs)* Jesus, you aren't a Conquistador at
all.

CONQUISTADOR: No.

BARBARA: Where did you get all the fancy armor?

CONQUISTADOR: I do not know. I only know I was in
it when I met you. And I had things in my head that
explained it.

BARBARA: Stories?

CONQUISTADOR: Yes.

BARBARA: You see this outfit I have on? I'm in prison.
What do you make of that? You show up and tell
me you're a killer and I get all inspired and stab my
husband with a carving knife.

CONQUISTADOR: You stabbed him with my sword.

BARBARA: That's not what they say.

CONQUISTADOR: Who?

BARBARA: The Inquisition! What does it matter what anyone calls themselves.

CONQUISTADOR: You are angry.

BARBARA: Yes. No. I was. Now I'm just jaded and world-weary.

CONQUISTADOR: A shepherd.

BARBARA: What?

CONQUISTADOR: A shepherd.

(*An Andalusian* SHEPHERD *[*GUITAR PLAYER*] is lit. He carries a staff and a guitar slung over his shoulder, on his back.*)

(BARBARA *and* CONQUISTADOR *look at him.*)

BARBARA: Jesus.

(SHEPHERD *points to his mouth and shakes his head.*)

CONQUISTADOR: He is mute.

BARBARA: He looks like John.

CONQUISTADOR: (*To* SHEPHERD) She is not from around here.

BARBARA: What is this place?

CONQUISTADOR: Andalusia.

BARBARA: What is this place to you?

CONQUISTADOR: My home.

BARBARA: Spain.

CONQUISTADOR: Yes.

BARBARA: This is Spain?

CONQUISTADOR: Welcome.

(SHEPHERD *hands off his staff to* CONQUISTADOR *and swings his guitar into playing position. He sings.*)

SHEPHERD: *Si mi corazón tuviera*
bierieritas e cristar,
te asomaras y lo vieras
gotas de sangre llorar.

(*Silence.* SHEPHERD *swings his guitar back over his shoulder and takes his staff back from* CONQUISTADOR. *He walks off.*)

BARBARA: I thought he was mute.

CONQUISTADOR: He is.

BARBARA: He has a very nice singing voice for a mute.

CONQUISTADOR: He sings the deep song.

BARBARA: It was charming.

CONQUISTADOR: *Siguiriya.*

BARBARA: I don't know Spanish.

CONQUISTADOR: "If my heart had windowpanes of glass, you'd look inside and see it crying drops of blood."

BARBARA: I'm feeling angry.

CONQUISTADOR: Why?

BARBARA: What the hell is going on here?

CONQUISTADOR: You are where you always wanted to be.

BARBARA: Stop. Why did I see blood on your sword if you didn't kill anyone?

CONQUISTADOR: It was not truly my sword.

BARBARA: What is your real name?

CONQUISTADOR: Pepe.

BARBARA: *(Disgusted)* God.

CONQUISTADOR: The discovery of the New World marked a major turning point in my life.

BARBARA: Excuse me?

CONQUISTADOR: Conquering. It is a great feeling.

BARBARA: Stop.

CONQUISTADOR: We go places and name them.

BARBARA: Stop. Why are you saying those things?

CONQUISTADOR: I said them before.

BARBARA: You're not a conquistador anymore.

CONQUISTADOR: The heart of Spain is gold.

BARBARA: Who the fuck are you?

CONQUISTADOR: It is a wind that blows over the heads of the dead.

BARBARA: What?

CONQUISTADOR: Duende.

BARBARA: What the fuck is Duende?

CONQUISTADOR: *Dónde está el duende?*

(A MONK *[*ANCIENT*] enters, dressed in a white robe and black scapular. New lighting, suggesting a church. The* MONK *gets into prayer position downstage.* BARBARA *and* CONQUISTADOR *watch him.)*

BARBARA: What happened?

CONQUISTADOR: Shhh. He is praying.

MONK: *Dominus padre om.*
Et spiritus sancti uno.
Duende, Duende, Duende.
Barbara, Barbara, Barbara.

BARBARA: What is this?

(Silence. MONK *turns and looks at* BARBARA. *Silence.*
He stands. He walks to her and places his hand over her
heart. She is frozen.)

MONK: *Dónde está el duende?*
What do you want?

(Silence. BARBARA *is in a trance.)*

BARBARA: I want faces made of glass. No more soft lips
or cheeks or baby smiles. I want sharp angles and grey
lines. I want eyes like lifeless diamonds. I want to live
touching nothing. I want to float invisible.

*(*MONK *holds out his arms, Christlike.* CONQUISTADOR
walks to him and disrobes him. Underneath his robe, MONK
is LAWYER. *Lights shift back to the way they were at the*
top of the act. Back in the little room with BARBARA *and*
LAWYER. CONQUISTADOR *and the* MONK's *robe are gone.)*

LAWYER: Barbara?

*(*BARBARA *stares at Lawyer.)*

LAWYER: Are you all right?

*(*BARBARA *laughs.)*

BARBARA: Now who are you?

LAWYER: I'm your lawyer. I think you just had some
sort of episode.

BARBARA: Several, actually.

LAWYER: You said some things.

BARBARA: I bet I did.

LAWYER: You said: faces made of glass. What does that
mean?

BARBARA: If my heart had windowpanes of glass.

LAWYER: Barbara, I think the next step is to bring in a
psychiatrist.

BARBARA: Will that be you, too?

LAWYER: I don't think we're going to have much trouble with the insanity plea.

BARBARA: What are all these pieces?

LAWYER: Pieces?

BARBARA: Monks and Mayans and Conquistadors.

LAWYER: Yes, I completely agree. I think perhaps our meeting is done for now.

BARBARA: What's next? You know? Donde esta el duende?

LAWYER: Absolutely. Nothing to worry about.

(MATADOR [JOHN] enters with a flourish. BARBARA collapses laughing.)

LAWYER: Yes. Keep laughing. That's wonderful. This is all on tape. Nothing to worry about at all.

(The MATADOR looks to be sizing up BARBARA as if she were a bull. She starts to play the role, making her fingers into horns and brushing the ground with her foot. LAWYER watches.)

LAWYER: Beautiful. That's...amazing. Keep going, don't stop.

(BARBARA charges MATADOR and gores him.)

(Lights shift to illuminate DIVERSION, dressed as a FLAMENCO DANCER. She dances in silence for a few moments. Then speaks and dances at the same time.)

DIVERSION: The funny thing is: I know Spanish. I've read Lorca backwards and forwards. I took Flamenco classes at the gym. But that was a phase, you know? I got over it and settled down. Now I have a steady job and pets and all the comfortable amenities of American life. So I suppose, really, I was as discouraging as John when it came to Barbara's obsession. I wanted her to get over it. It only reminded me of a way I used to be. Young. How depressing. Younger. Than now. Now I see a shrink and pay my bills on time.

(Lights shift.)

*(*CONQUISTADOR *leads* BARBARA *along a narrow cliff ledge.)*

CONQUISTADOR: Careful. It is a great distance down from this cliff.

BARBARA: Where are we going?

CONQUISTADOR: To the valley. Over that stream. Through those woods.

BARBARA: What is our destination?

CONQUISTADOR: My home.

BARBARA: Your house.

CONQUISTADOR: We must get there before dark.

BARBARA: What happens after dark?

CONQUISTADOR: Wolves.

BARBARA: It's strange. You're nothing like you were, but it's still you.

CONQUISTADOR: We will also have to pass through a waterfall. Up ahead, beyond that ridge.

BARBARA: Do I seem different?

CONQUISTADOR: It is always hard to understand you.

BARBARA: Other than that.

CONQUISTADOR: Yes. You keep changing.

BARBARA: Are you sad that you aren't a Conquistador anymore?

CONQUISTADOR: A little. I am glad we could meet again.

BARBARA: Oh? Why is that?

CONQUISTADOR: You help me to understand myself.

BARBARA: Oh.

CONQUISTADOR: Come. We are nearly to the waterfall.

(They exit.)

(Light to DIVERSION, *no longer dancing, just fanning herself.)*

DIVERSION: I used to watch her at her desk. She'd stare off into space, stare like she saw something there. And then she'd come to me with her latest map or picture, some story she found, some word. I would pretend I didn't know what the words were, pretend the fantasies she had didn't used to be my own. You reach a point where fantasizing like that is just embarrassing. When it's time to look at where you really are. *(She looks down at her fan. She walks off.*

*(*CONQUISTADOR *and* BARBARA *enter. This is now* CONQUISTADOR's *home. A mat for sleeping, not much else.)*

BARBARA: This is where you live?

CONQUISTADOR: Yes.

(Beat)

BARBARA: I like it.

CONQUISTADOR: It is not soft like your house.

BARBARA: That's fine.

CONQUISTADOR: Would you like to sit?

*(*CONQUISTADOR *gestures.* BARBARA *sits. She looks at him, he looks at her.)*

CONQUISTADOR: Are you thirsty?

BARBARA: Yes.

CONQUISTADOR: Wait here.

*(*CONQUISTADOR *disappears.* BARBARA *is alone.)*

BARBARA: *(Calling for him)* El Tigre? Pepe?

(CONQUISTADOR appears with two clay cups full of mead and a rolled-up piece of parchment. He sets everything down and sits.)

CONQUISTADOR: I have something to show you.
(He unrolls the parchment. It is a drawing of a conquistador on horseback.)

BARBARA: A Conquistador. Did you draw that?

CONQUISTADOR: No. It was given to me. Do you want to hear the story?

BARBARA: Is it true? Never mind, that doesn't even matter. Tell me the story.

CONQUISTADOR: I was out in the fields.

BARBARA: The lush green countryside.

CONQUISTADOR: The fields of the farm. It was planting season.

BARBARA: Of course.

CONQUISTADOR: A shadow fell over me while I bent to the earth. I looked up to see a man dressed as I have never seen a man dressed.

(GENERAL [ANCIENT] appears. He is dressed in a white uniform, a purple sash, white gloves, medals on his chest and sunglasses.)

CONQUISTADOR: I asked him who he was.

GENERAL: General Don Enrique Briz Armengol.

CONQUISTADOR: I asked him where he was from?

GENERAL: Tierra de los Muertos.

CONQUISTADOR: He held out this parchment for me to take. I stood and unrolled it. The sun glowed brown off the earth. I saw this. What is this?

GENERAL: Conquistador.

CONQUISTADOR: And he told me what that meant.
He spoke of the New World. Of Savages. Of noble
knights on horseback claiming the land from a people
destined to be conquered. Of their ladies and their
power. I asked him if he was one of them.

GENERAL: No. *(Walks away.)*

CONQUISTADOR: And then the sun grew big in the sky
and his white clothes blinded my eyes. When I could
see again, he was gone. I was left alone in the fields
with this.
    When I returned home that night, I looked at it again.
I studied it for hours. Sometimes I could hear the sound
in my head of horses' hoofs stomping or of victory
cries. I could hear fire crackling. I smelled smoke.
And when I put my face close, I could see a shape
carefully drawn on the helmet.

BARBARA: A tiger.

CONQUISTADOR: Yes.

BARBARA: I used to sit at my desk at work and make
lists of cities. Spanish cities. Barcelona, Madrid, San
Sebastían: I looked them up, collected pictures. I made
a book of the pictures. The cathedrals, the rolling
golden hills, people laughing and drinking, playing
guitars, dancing flamenco, always lit by fire all around
them; people living unafraid of anything, so full of
passion and life and—

CONQUISTADOR: Duende!

BARBARA: Duende.

CONQUISTADOR: Burning coals.

BARBARA: Boiling blood.

CONQUISTADOR: Purpose.

BARBARA: Action.

CONQUISTADOR: In my guts.

BARBARA: Down my spine.

CONQUISTADOR: In my center.

BARBARA: In my soul. *(Pause)* You said I helped you understand yourself. What did you mean?
  How did I help you?

CONQUISTADOR: You were a better Conquistador than I ever could be.
  You made me remember my true self.
  That is who I am now.

BARBARA: *(They drink.)* You wanted to sleep with me. Was that as the Conquistador or as you? *(Silence)*
Don't be embarrassed.

CONQUISTADOR: I grew excited when I touched you.

BARBARA: Obviously. It excited me a little, too.

CONQUISTADOR: Truly?

BARBARA: A little. It also disturbed me. I haven't been touched by a man other than my husband in many years. And when he touched me, it wasn't the way that you touched me. Even though his hands were warm and yours were cold.

CONQUISTADOR: I have never been so bold with a woman.

BARBARA: Have you ever been with a woman? *(Silence)*
  It's all right.
  This drink is good. What is it?

CONQUISTADOR: Mead.

BARBARA: You made it yourself, didn't you?

CONQUISTADOR: Yes.

(BARBARA *smiles.*)

CONQUISTADOR: What is it? Why are you smiling?

BARBARA: I really like you.

(*Silence.* BARBARA *leans across and kisses* CONQUISTADOR *gently on the lips. She pulls back.*)

BARBARA: Have you ever felt that?

(CONQUISTADOR *bows his head.*)

BARBARA: Did it feel good?

CONQUISTADOR: Yes.

BARBARA: You're shivering.
    Close your eyes.

(CONQUISTADOR *does.* BARBARA *kisses him again, holding him to her.*)

(*The* LAWYER *appears reading off a legal pad.*)

LAWYER: I want faces made of glass, no more soft lips or baby smiles. Sharp angles, gray lines. Eyes like lifeless diamonds. Floating invisible. Barbara?

BARBARA: Go away.

(CONQUISTADOR *stops.* BARBARA *pulls him back to her.*)

BARBARA: Not you.

(LAWYER *exits.*)

(*More kissing, lights dim on* CONQUISTADOR *and* BARBARA.)

(DIVERSION *appears in a separate space in her Flamenco dress, slipping it off as she talks. Underneath she wears a simple white slip. Her tone reflects this.*)

DIVERSION: It was so familiar. Her desire. It was something that I thought had died in me. That I had perhaps killed. And it was dangerous, I knew it was, to be near her, because what if that thing I killed had not died and came back and made me do...something like what she did? It would be so easy. To wake up one morning, take all the money out of the bank, tell Roman to go to hell, buy a plane ticket or a train ticket or just drive away, give up everything I'd decided was important. Find a beach somewhere, steal a horse, ride it along the waves, poor red sangria down my throat while I rode, pour it all over my face. *(She exits.)*

BARBARA: Scratchy face.

CONQUISTADOR: What?

BARBARA: Your beard. Scratchy face. It's nice.

CONQUISTADOR: Thank you.

BARBARA: Do you know what to do next?

CONQUISTADOR: Next?

BARBARA: Touch me the way you touched me before.

(CONQUISTADOR does so. They are still.)

BARBARA: It's different.

(CONQUISTADOR withdraws his hand. BARBARA takes it and puts it back where it was.)

BARBARA: It's better.

(BARBARA pulls CONQUISTADOR down to make love.

(DIVERSION, in her slip, rides through on the back of a HORSE [GUITAR PLAYER]. She surveys the landscape.)

(The ANCIENT appears across the stage with a bottle of sangria, holds it out to DIVERSION, who rides towards her unquestioningly, like in a dream. She grabs up the bottle and drinks as she rides around and off.)

(Lights rise on CONQUISTADOR and BARBARA, lying in bed together, entwined peacefully.)

BARBARA: How do you feel?

CONQUISTADOR: Uhhh...

BARBARA: Good. That's good. You're a man, that's how you're supposed to feel.

CONQUISTADOR: How did it feel to you?

BARBARA: Good. Thank you for asking. You're a wonderful lover.

CONQUISTADOR: I do not remember doing anything.

BARBARA: You responded to everything I did. You cared about me.

CONQUISTADOR: Barbara?

BARBARA: Yes.

CONQUISTADOR: Why did you do this?

BARBARA: Because I wanted to.

CONQUISTADOR: What do we do now?

BARBARA: We lie here like this. You hold me and I feel your warmth around me. We breathe together. We tell each other how lucky we are. We talk about anything, it doesn't matter what. We look into each other's eyes and find peace, amazing peace and relief. You tell me you love my lips. I tell you I love how your arms feel around me. We make plans for the day, or the night, or the next day. We make plans for our life together. We make so many plans.

CONQUISTADOR: You are crying. Are you sad?

BARBARA: No.

CONQUISTADOR: Your husband.

BARBARA: No, it's not him.

CONQUISTADOR: Your husband.

(CONQUISTADOR *is looking at* JOHN, *who stands near the bed, simply watching.* BARBARA *follows* CONQUISTADOR's *gaze.* JOHN *wears his blood-stained clothes. He is holding the Spanish sword. He and* BARBARA *stare at each other.)*

BARBARA: What are you doing here?

JOHN: I remember the way we started out.
  We used to go for long walks holding hands, swinging them. And then I would pull you to me and kiss you and the wind would blow your hair all over your face and I'd brush it away and kiss you again.
  And the first time we were naked together and you touched me and you pulled me into you and your lips parted like an O and you sighed so softly. And the first time you told me you loved me and I loved you.
  What is he doing here?

BARBARA: None of your business.

JOHN: Big muscles and no neck.

BARBARA: No.

JOHN: You replaced me with him.

BARBARA: You left me.

JOHN: I'm back.

BARBARA: You're dead.

(JOHN raises the sword.)

BARBARA: What are you doing? What can you possibly do?

(JOHN quickly stabs CONQUISTADOR.*)*

BARBARA: No! NO!

CONQUISTADOR: Barbara...

JOHN: Barbara...

*(*BARBARA *grabs the sword away from* JOHN *by the blade. She looks at* CONQUISTADOR, *who looks up at her. She looks at* JOHN, *who sinks to his knees before her and dies.)*

(BARBARA *goes to and holds* CONQUISTADOR. *He is dying.*)

BARBARA: Please no, not you, no...

CONQUISTADOR: Barbara...

BARBARA: I'm right here, it's okay, you're fine

CONQUISTADOR: My blood...I am dying.

BARBARA: No, you are not, this can't happen.

CONQUISTADOR: I am going quickly...

BARBARA: No, you can't die!

CONQUISTADOR: The heart of Spain...

BARBARA: No, no, no you don't...

CONQUISTADOR: Red and black and yellow...

BARBARA: Stay with me.

CONQUISTADOR: The New World, the new me...

BARBARA: Please don't leave me.

CONQUISTADOR: *(Suddenly very calm, knowing)* Barbara.

(BARBARA *looks at* CONQUISTADOR.)

CONQUISTADOR: This is what I was made for.
    You have so much... *(He dies.)*

BARBARA: *(Weakly)* Wait...

(He's gone.)

(BARBARA *holds* CONQUISTADOR.)

(A deep drum pounds offstage. It starts into a rhythmic pattern building in intensity.)

(Gradually, orange and red light rises upstage. In the light a figure can be made out.... DIVERSION. *She is naked [literally or gesturally]; holds a long piece of red fabric that she trails behind her.)*

(BARBARA *looks at her, cradling* CONQUISTADOR.)

(DIVERSION looks back at her.)

(BARBARA lays CONQUISTADOR down gently.)

(She stands, not taking her eyes off DIVERSION.)

(She walks towards her.)

(DIVERSION suddenly runs at BARBARA, the red cloth flying behind her. She reaches BARBARA and starts a wild chaotic dance, using the red cloth in her movement to create swooping, billowing movement, enveloping BARBARA. Lights and drumming are very loud. Chaos, bright and disorienting. BARBARA stands at the center of it, overwhelmed.)

(Blackout)

(Lights quickly rise on the ANCIENT, sitting in a separate space, beating a lone drum with slow intensity. BARBARA enters his space, reminiscent of the CONQUISTADOR's first encounter with ANCIENT.)

(She stands before him.)

ANCIENT: *Buenas noches.*

BARBARA: Good evening.

ANCIENT: *Noches.*

BARBARA: Night.

ANCIENT: *Sí.*

BARBARA: Who are you?

(ANCIENT smiles.)

BARBARA: I don't understand who you are.

(The ANCIENT's smile disappears.)

BARBARA: I don't understand who I am.

(The ANCIENT nods.)

BARBARA: Can this just stop for second? Can we just hold still for a second?

ANCIENT: Sí.

(Stillness)

(BARBARA looks around the stage.)

(Lights have come up. DIVERSION, wrapped in the red cloth, now stands near the bodies of JOHN and CONQUISTADOR.)

ANCIENT: Do you know who *they* are?

(BARBARA nods.)

ANCIENT: Tell it.

(BARBARA gathers her strength; she goes to JOHN's body.)

BARBARA: This is my husband. His name was John. He played guitar. He used to kiss me on the back of my neck. He would part my hair and press his warm lips...here.
  He fell in love with another woman. He fell out of love with me. *(She takes this in and turns to the body of CONQUISTADOR.)*
  And this is the Conquistador. His name is Pepe. He kills people. He loves himself. He makes everything up and he makes his own liquor.
  I fell in love with him. I fell out of love with my husband.
  They killed each other. I killed both of them.

(ANCIENT beats two heart pulses on his drum. BARBARA turns. DIVERSION has moved to her side. BARBARA looks at her.)

BARBARA: This is Diversion. My best friend, Diversion. She pretends she doesn't know. She pretents she dreamt it all. She killed her soul. This is her soul.

(ANCIENT beats another heart pulse. BARBARA looks at him.)

BARBARA: This is a textbook. This is the man in charge.
This is a lunatic. This is everything I know. This is
madness.

(ANCIENT *beats the drum again.* BARBARA *becomes aware
of the audience.*)

(*She takes us in.*)

BARBARA: This is a woman alone in her living room.
This is a human being alone. (*Silence. She breathes.*)
    Can I just be alone? Please? Please.

(BARBARA *closes her eyes. The* ANCIENT *starts a drum roll.*

(*Diversion disappears.*)

(CONQUISTADOR *and* JOHN *rise. They take off the bed
together. They bring in the sofa from 1 together and set it
where it was. They take off the chairs. They bring on the
coffee table.* BARBARA *keeps her eyes shut. They all leave.*)

(BARBARA *is alone in her living room. Silence. She looks
around.*)

(*She sits on the sofa. She puts her feet up on the coffee table.
She breathes.*)

(*A doorbell. Silence*)

BARBARA: Come in.

(DIVERSION *enters, dressed normally.*)

DIVERSION: Hi.

BARBARA: Hi.

DIVERSION: Are you all right?

BARBARA: Yeah. Sit down here by me.

(DIVERSION *does so.*)

BARBARA: Put your feet up on the table.

(DIVERSION *does so.*)

DIVERSION: Barbara. Did something happen?

BARBARA: John left.

DIVERSION: What?

BARBARA: John left me for some woman he fell in love with.

DIVERSION: Barbara...

BARBARA: It's all right.

DIVERSION: All right? He left you. Aren't you devastated?

BARBARA: No.

DIVERSION: But you're all alone. It's terrible.

BARBARA: I'm going to take a trip.

DIVERSION: Spain?

BARBARA: Yes.

DIVERSION: You don't speak Spanish.

BARBARA: I'll learn.

(Blackout)

END OF PLAY